LEOPARD SEAL VS. COUGAR

Gareth Stevens
PUBLISHING

By Natalie Humphrey

Please visit our website, www.garethstevens.com. For a free color catalog of all our high-quality books, call toll free 1-800-542-2595 or fax 1-877-542-2596.

Library of Congress Cataloging-in-Publication Data
Names: Humphrey, Natalie, author.
Title: Leopard seal vs. cougar / Natalie Humphrey.
Other titles: Leopard seal versus cougar
Description: New York : Gareth Stevens Publishing, [2023] | Series: Bizarre
    beast battles | Includes bibliographical references and index. |
    Identifiers: LCCN 2022029416 | ISBN 9781538284070 (paperback) | ISBN
    9781538284094 (library binding) | ISBN 9781538284100 (ebook)
Subjects: LCSH: Leopard seal–Juvenile literature. | Puma–Juvenile
    literature.
Classification: LCC QL737.P64 H86 2023 | DDC 599.75/24–dc23/eng/20220707
LC record available at https://lccn.loc.gov/2022029416

First Edition

Published in 2023 by
Gareth Stevens Publishing
2544 Clinton Street
Buffalo, NY 14224

Designer: Leslie Taylor
Editor: Natalie Humphrey

Photo credits: Cover (cougar) Phil Silverman/Shutterstock.com; cover (seal) Marcos Amend/Shutterstock.com; series art (background texture) Apostrophe/Shutterstock.com; series art (seal icon) Olga Potter/Shutterstock.com; series art (cougar icon) Forgem/Shutterstock.com; pgs. 4 and 6 Andrei Minsk/Shutterstock.com; p. 5 SZakharov/Shutterstock.com; p. 7 Evgeniyqw/Shutterstock.com; p. 8 Mogens Trolle/Shutterstock.com; p. 9 sirtravelalot/Shutterstock.com; p. 10 Radharc Images/Alamy.com; p. 11 taviphoto/Shutterstock.com; p. 12 MZPHOTO.CZ/Shutterstock.com; p. 13 Michal Ninger/Shutterstock.com; p. 14 buenaventura/Shutterstock.com; p. 15 Danita Delimont/Shutterstock.com; p. 16 Justin Hofman/Alamy.com; p. 17 AB Photographie/Shutterstock.com; p. 18 slowmotiongli/Shutterstock.com; p. 19 JoeFotos/Shutterstock.com; p. 21 (seal) Tarpan/Shutterstock.com; p. 21 (cougar) Evgeniyqw/Shutterstock.com.

Printed in the United States of America

CPSIA compliance information: Batch #CWGS23: For further information contact Gareth Stevens at 1-800-542-2595.

CONTENTS

Words in the glossary appear in **bold** type the first time they are used in the text.

TERROR UNDERWATER

In the cold waters near Antarctica, the leopard seal waits for its **prey**. This predator prefers to hide near the shore, waiting for penguins to jump in or out of the water. Then, the leopard seal quickly chomps its meal! Using its strong **jaws** and sharp teeth, the leopard seal can catch undersea prey. Fast and deadly, the leopard seal is one strange beast that could easily beat most other animals.

But is it strong enough to win in a battle against a cougar?

LEOPARD SEAL **RANGE**

ANTARCTICA

THE LEOPARD SEAL'S LONG, THIN BODY HELPS IT MOVE QUICKLY UNDERWATER.

5

THE MOUNTAIN HUNTER

The cougar is a beast with many names. They are also known as mountain lions and pumas. This predator is perfectly **adapted** to its wild homes in North, Central, and South America. Some cougars live on rocky mountainsides while others live in the desert. Though their natural North American home has shrunk because of **habitat** changes and hunting, the cougar is a tough competitor.

But is this fearless **feline** strong enough to beat a leopard seal?

NORTH AMERICA

CENTRAL AMERICA

SOUTH AMERICA

COUGAR RANGE
 Today (approximate)   Pre-European settlement

COUGARS ARE STRONG HUNTERS
ANYWHERE THEY LIVE.

7

THE BIGGEST HUNTER

Leopard seals are one of the biggest types of seal, but are they bigger than cougars? Leopard seals have long, heavy bodies that move quickly underwater. This cold-water beast has a thick layer of **blubber** that keeps it warm in the coldest conditions.

LEOPARD SEAL

- LENGTH: 10 TO 12 FEET (3 TO 4 m)
- WEIGHT: 661 TO 1,100 POUNDS (300 TO 500 kg)

COUGAR
- LENGTH: 7 TO 8 FEET (2 TO 2.4 m)
- WEIGHT: 64 TO 264 POUNDS (29 TO 120 KG)

Cougars are the second largest big cat in North and South America. They have powerful legs and big paws. But in a battle of sizes, a cougar can't compare to the leopard seal's huge size!

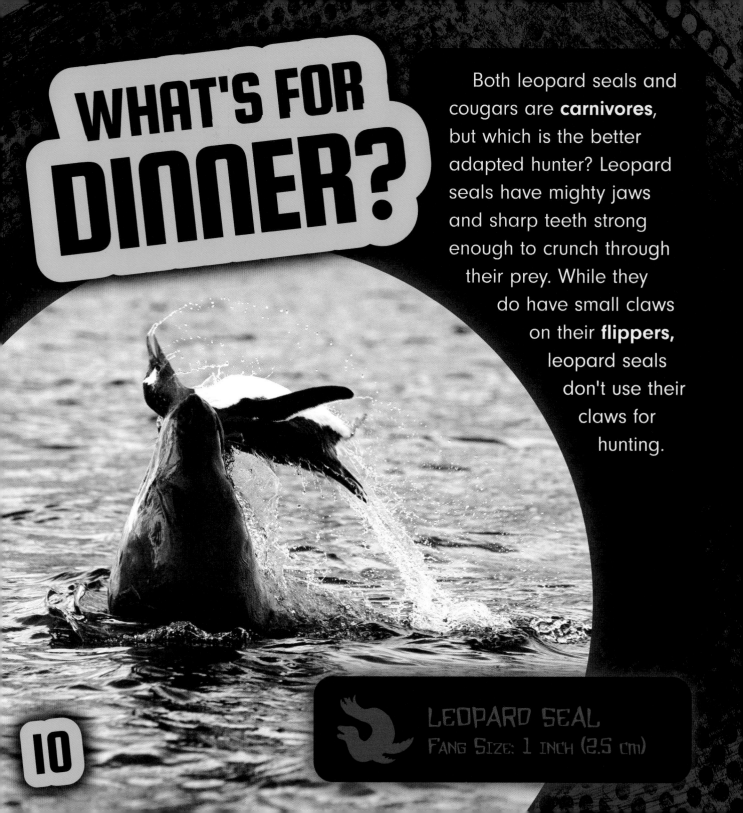

WHAT'S FOR DINNER?

Both leopard seals and cougars are **carnivores**, but which is the better adapted hunter? Leopard seals have mighty jaws and sharp teeth strong enough to crunch through their prey. While they do have small claws on their **flippers,** leopard seals don't use their claws for hunting.

LEOPARD SEAL
FANG SIZE: 1 INCH (2.5 cm)

COUGAR
FANG SIZE: 1.5 TO 2 INCHES (4 TO 5 cm)

Between a leopard seal and a cougar, a cougar has much larger fangs and claws. A cougar's claws are used to hold onto their prey while their fangs bite into the back of their prey's neck. Because both its fangs and claws are bigger, the cougar wins!

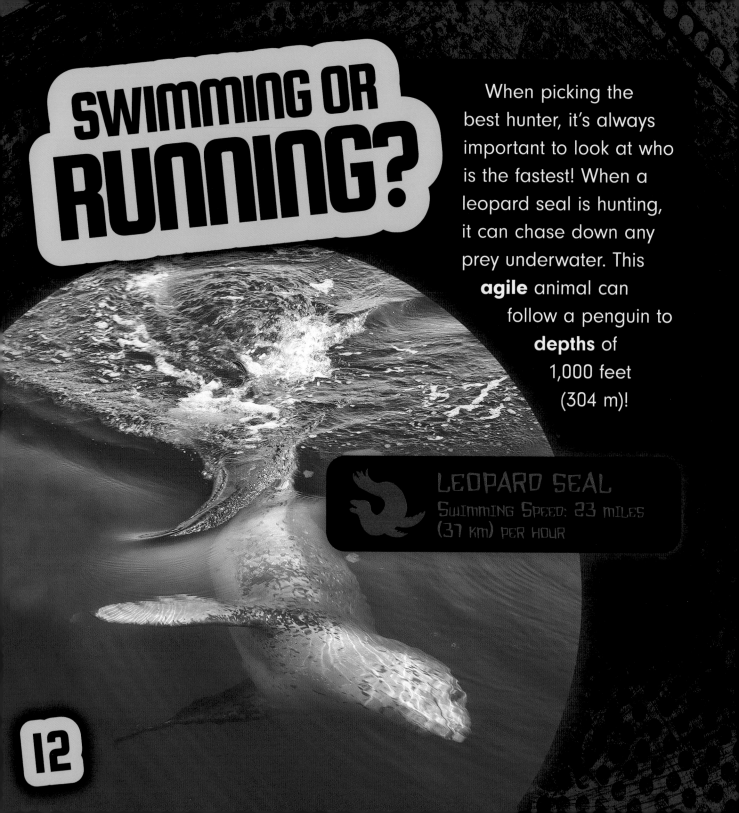

SWIMMING OR RUNNING?

When picking the best hunter, it's always important to look at who is the fastest! When a leopard seal is hunting, it can chase down any prey underwater. This **agile** animal can follow a penguin to **depths** of 1,000 feet (304 m)!

LEOPARD SEAL
Swimming Speed: 23 miles (37 km) per hour

COUGAR
RUNNING SPEED: UP TO
50 MILES (80.5 KM) PER HOUR

Cougars also swim to catch their prey, but they would rather run! Because their favorite prey is fast, mountain lions need to be faster. At top speed, a mountain lion can outrun a deer or even a car! The cougar has the leopard seal beat in this battle.

13

HOW MANY ARE THERE?

Leopard seals live on **ice floes,** but as the water gets warmer, these ice floes are melting. A major threat, or danger, leopard seals face is **climate change**! Their population is large, but it could decrease if Earth keeps warming up.

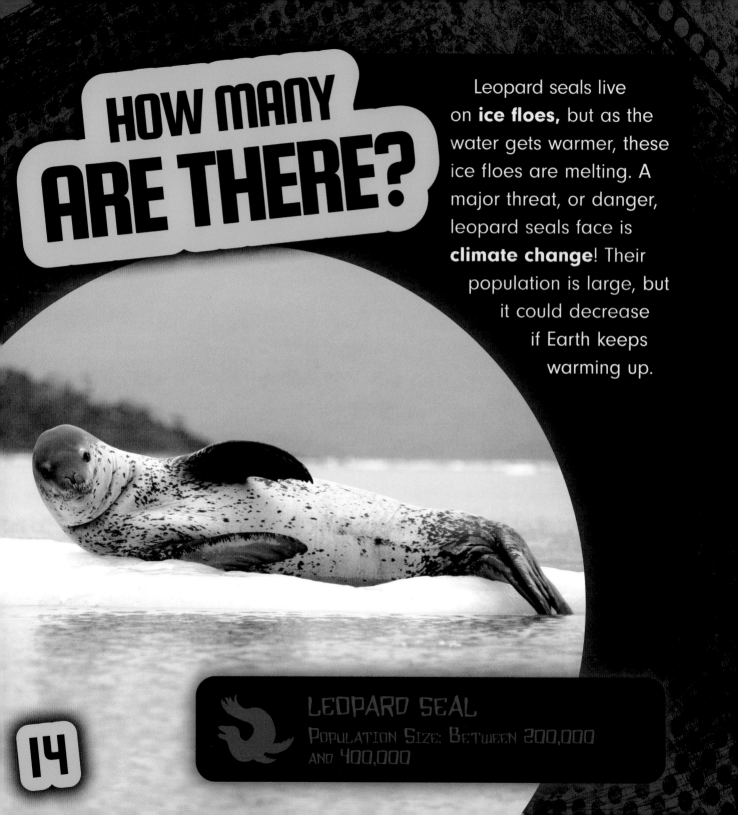

LEOPARD SEAL
POPULATION SIZE: BETWEEN 200,000 AND 400,000

Even though the number of cougars left in the United States is less than the total number of leopard seals, the winner of this battle isn't clear. We don't know exactly how many cougars live outside of the United States, so it's hard to

COUGAR
U.S. POPULATION SIZE:
20,000 TO 40,000

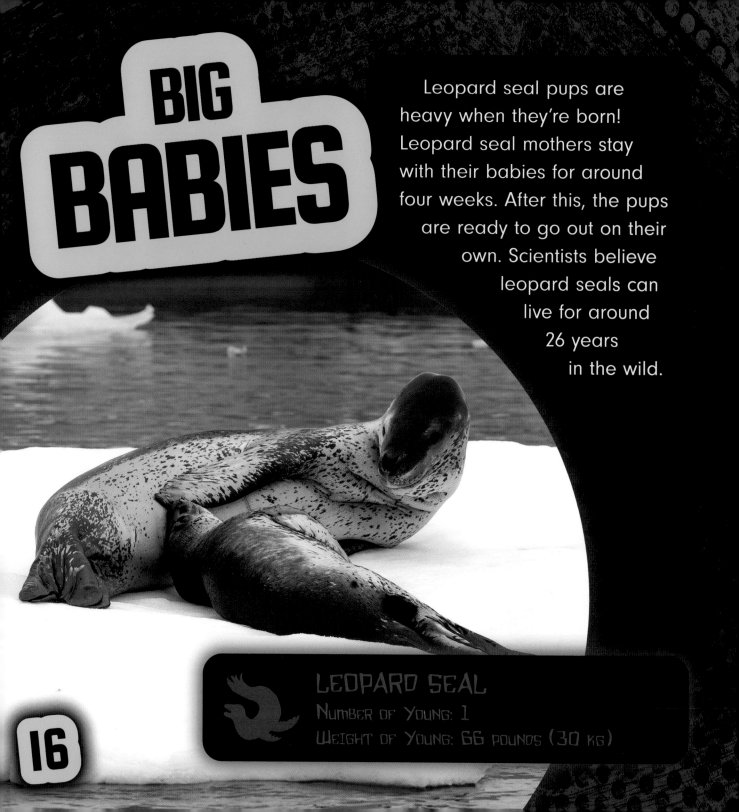

BIG BABIES

Leopard seal pups are heavy when they're born! Leopard seal mothers stay with their babies for around four weeks. After this, the pups are ready to go out on their own. Scientists believe leopard seals can live for around 26 years in the wild.

LEOPARD SEAL
Number of Young: 1
Weight of Young: 66 pounds (30 kg)

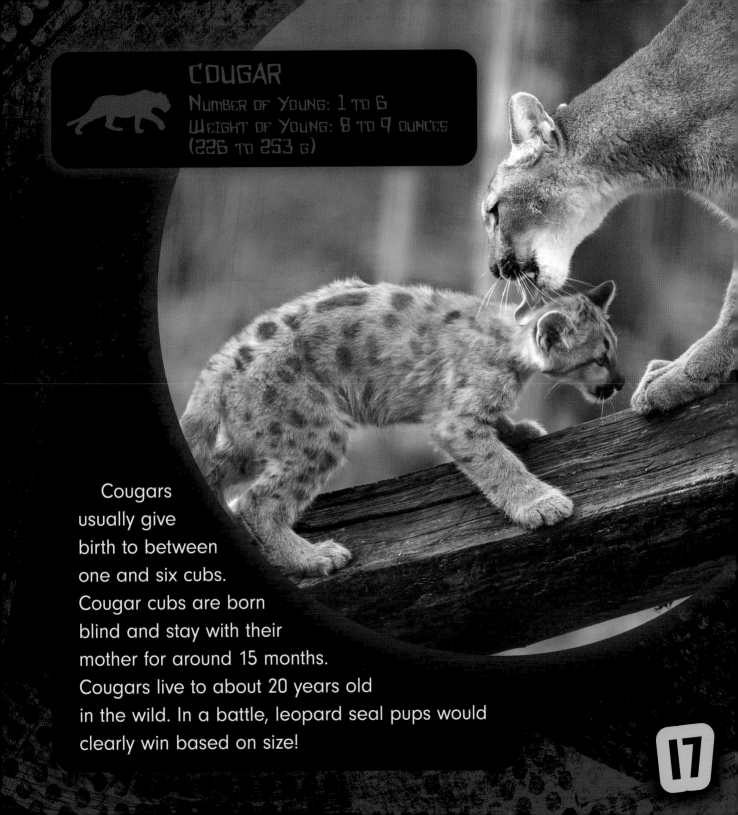

COUGAR
Number of Young: 1 to 6
Weight of Young: 8 to 9 ounces
(226 to 253 g)

Cougars usually give birth to between one and six cubs. Cougar cubs are born blind and stay with their mother for around 15 months. Cougars live to about 20 years old in the wild. In a battle, leopard seal pups would clearly win based on size!

17

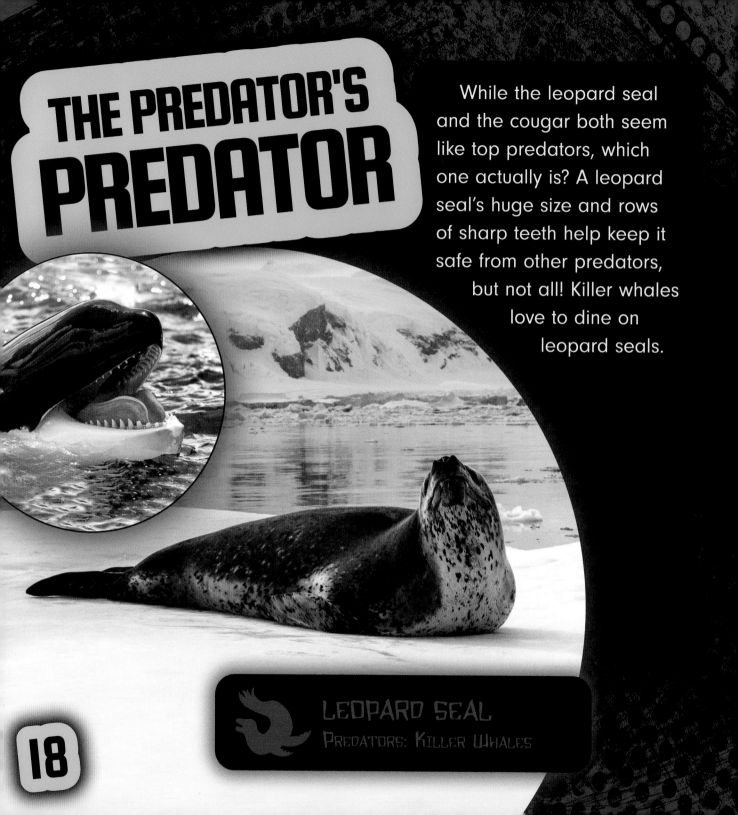

THE PREDATOR'S PREDATOR

While the leopard seal and the cougar both seem like top predators, which one actually is? A leopard seal's huge size and rows of sharp teeth help keep it safe from other predators, but not all! Killer whales love to dine on leopard seals.

LEOPARD SEAL
PREDATORS: KILLER WHALES

COUGAR

PREDATORS: NONE, BUT MAY COMPETE WITH BLACK BEARS FOR FOOD IN SOME PARTS OF ITS RANGE

Unlike the leopard seal, the cougar is usually at the top of its food chain! The cougar is known as an apex predator in parts of its range. Apex predators are animals that hunt other animals, but no animal hunts them. The cougar wins this battle!

19

WHO WOULD WIN?

In a battle between these two top predators, it's hard to pick who would win! Would the leopard seal be able to outswim the cougar, or would the cougar outrun the seal?

Could the cougar use its adaptability to get out of trouble? Or would the huge size of the leopard seal be too much to handle? How would a leopard seal's strong bite match up against the cougar's sharp teeth? Who do you think would win?

 THESE TWO ANIMALS LIVE IN VERY DIFFERENT PLACES IN THE WILD, SO A MATCHUP BETWEEN THEM WOULD BE A SHOCKING BATTLE!

GLOSSARY

adapt: To change to suit conditions. Adaptability is the ability to change to suit conditions.

agile: Able to move quickly and easily.

blubber: A thick layer of fat found on some mammals.

carnivore: An animal that eats meat.

climate change: Long-term change in Earth's climate, caused by human activities such as burning oil and natural gas.

depth: The distance between something and the surface of water.

feline: The name for the cat family.

flipper: A wide, flat "arm" used for swimming.

habitat: The natural place where an animal or plant lives.

ice floe: Flat pieces of ice floating in the ocean.

jaws: The bones that hold the teeth and make up the mouth.

prey: An animal that is hunted by other animals for food.

range: The area where something lives.

FOR MORE INFORMATION

BOOKS

Adamson, Thomas K. *Mountain Lion vs. Coyote*. Minneapolis, MN: Bellwether Media, 2021.

Hansen, Grace. *Leopard Seal*. Minneapolis, MN: Abdo Kids, 2022.

WEBSITES

A-Z Animals: Leopard Seal
a-z-animals.com/animals/leopard-seal/
Check out more fun facts about how leopard seals live in the cold wild.

San Diego Zoo Wildlife Explorers: Mountain Lion
sdzwildlifeexplorers.org/animals/mountain-lion
Discover more interesting facts and fun videos about mountain lions.

INDEX